Moments of Reflection

Prayers and Affirmations

To Accompany Essential Oils

By

Jennie Fuller

This book is dedicated to God for the gift of the plants and oils and to D. Gary Young and Mary Young for bringing these beautiful oils to us.

Table of Contents

Prayers with Single Oils

Affirmations

Introduction

This book synergizes the power of prayer and affirmations with the power of essential oils. Essential oils range in frequency from 52 MHz to 580 MHz. Praying while applying essential oils increases the frequency of the oil by up to 15 MHz. Adding positive thoughts on average increases frequency up to 15 MHz. Combining prayer, essential oils, and positive words/thoughts can help maintain a high frequency.

I offer this book as a way to use the oils each day, while taking time to pray and connect with God as the oils are applied. The prayers are short to encourage daily use. If you only have a few seconds, to just apply the oils, I highly encourage that also, as the oils have amazing benefits on their own.

In addition to prayer, affirmations are a quick way to focus your thoughts on the positive throughout the day. Pairing essential oils and affirmations helps shift and redirect your thoughts. Since they are one sentence or phrase, it's easy to repeat them throughout the day. Even if you just have a couple seconds you can inhale one of the oils with an affirmation.

You could also anchor the affirmation with an essential oil in the morning, and take one or both with you for the day. The oil greatly assists in breaking old patterns, so being able to inhale (or apply) it is important.

To bring positive change into your life and live your highest potential, you need to focus your energy and thoughts on positive things. What you put your energy and thoughts on, attracts more of the same things. Thoughts and energy have frequencies, which attract more of the same frequency. Once you start to increase your frequency, the universe supports you more (and/or you will be able to easily see the support and love around you).

In addition to positive thoughts/affirmations, you want to align your emotions with the positive thought. Bring to mind a happy memory or picture someone or something you love. Feel that emotion in your body, and inhale the oil while thinking or saying the affirmation. Infuse the affirmation with that feeling. This is the key to bringing it into reality. For example, if I'm working with the affirmation "I choose to be happy", I'm going to inhale or apply an oil, while feeling happiness, joy, or love in my body while I focus on that affirmation.

Also feel free to customize the affirmations, and create new ones to use. You want to keep them positive and simple. The subconscious doesn't understand you saying "I do not want to eat sugar". It translates into "I want to eat sugar". Replace what it is that you want to change. "I choose honey (or stevia) for a sweetener", "I upgrade my sweetener", or "I choose, whole nourishing foods" would affirm the shift that you want. A simple direct statement also makes it easy for the subconscious mind to understand what you want. You want both your conscious mind and subconscious mind working together for maximum and noticeable results. You can also say "I am in the process of" at the front of an affirmation that is something you are reaching towards. Take steps towards what you want to bring into your life. An example of this would be "I am in the process of having extra money", "I have extra money left after each paycheck", "I have an extra $50 left each week", "I have an extra $100 left each week". Start with one that is believable to you and shift your vibration up into the next higher amount until it's comfortable, and then shift up again. It should give you positive angel bumps (goosebumps) or a similar feeling when it's the right one for the moment.

I recommend using Young Living Essential Oils. Young Living Essential Oils have a high frequency and purity. It's important to keep your body and energy field at a high frequency. Using Young Living Essential Oils can help maintain a high frequency. They are the only essential oils I've experienced that I can feel the energy and vitality of the oils – just from holding the bottle of oil. Young Living Essential Oils contain warmth, vitality, and aliveness that you want when using essential oils. There is love in every drop. More information on the quality of Young Living Essential Oils can be found at www.seedtoseal.com

It's extremely important to use a high quality essential oil for any use – topical, diffusion, or internal. You want to breathe in or apply the therapeutic qualities of the plant oil, not chemicals or synthetic fragrances and possible carcinogens that can be in low quality oils and synthetic fragrances.

Please check the labels on the oils for the recommended use. Oils can be diffused during prayer to enhance the environment. Frankincense or Sacred Frankincense is lovely for diffusing (and applying) during prayer and meditation. Oils that are safe to apply topically can be applied with a prayer to intensify the effect.

Typical points to apply the oils on the skin are bottom of the feet, ankles, wrists, and back of neck. They can also be applied over your stomach and other areas. Be careful with the "hot" oils such as oregano. It's best to dilute "hot" oils with a carrier oil, such as Young Living's V6 Vegetable Oil Complex or coconut oil, before applying them topically, especially the first few times. Please refer to the *Gentle Babies* book or the *Essential Oils Desk Reference* book for topical application of oils for children.

If you do not have the specific oil listed with a prayer or affirmation, feel free to use the oil you have available. Lavender can be used for almost all topics. It's a very intuitive and adaptable essential oil.

One way to select oils is to hold your hand over the oils and feel which oil(s) responds to you. I get angel bumps (goosebumps) on my arms or the back of my neck tingles when an oil resonates with me. If you do not have the oils present, you can also read the descriptions of the oils in the Young Living catalog and tune in to which ones resonate with you. You can also look up typical uses of oils in the *Essential Oils Desk Reference* book.

Another aspect to consider that can assist the effect of the oils is clean eating - cutting out processed food, fast food, processed sugar, etc. Removing chemicals from your food, cleaning products, beauty products, and personal care products cleanses you and your living space. Young Living has nontoxic skin care, personal care, and cleaning products infused with essential oils. Using natural and pure products also supports a high frequency living space.

One additional benefit of keeping your frequency and your living space at a high frequency is that our DNA responds to frequency. A high frequency may support DNA.

Prayers for Specific Topics

Abundance

Dear God,

Please guide this oil through my physical body and energy field. Raise my frequency to abundant prosperity. Please help me to attract and accept an abundance of love, joy, friendship, fulfillment, and money.

In Jesus' name, I pray.

Amen.

Suggested Oils: Abundance, Ginger, Orange

Dear God,

Please guide this oil through my body to each cell. Thank You for the abundance of love, joy, friendship, and prosperity that You have blessed me with.

In Jesus' name, I pray.

Amen.

Suggested Oils: Abundance, Gratitude

Acceptance

Dear God,

Please guide this oil through my physical body and energy field. Help me to accept all aspects of my life, and be in harmony with all of Your creation.

In Jesus' name, I pray.

Amen.

Suggested Oils: Acceptance, Harmony, Rose

Alignment - Body

Dear God,

Please guide this oil through my body and energy field. Calm my mind. Bring peace to my heart. Restore alignment to all aspects of my body and being.

In Jesus' name, I pray.

Amen.

Suggested Oils: Raindrop Collection, Valor, Valor II

Alignment - Life

Dear God,

Please guide this oil through my body and energy field to help bring my body, mind, and heart into harmony and unity. Align me with the flow of life. Help me to connect with my higher purpose for this lifetime.

In Jesus' name, I pray.

Amen.

Suggested Oils: Grounding, Highest Potential, Magnify Your Purpose, Valor, Valor II

Appreciation

Dear God,

Please guide this oil through my physical body and energy field. Help me to see all of the blessings in my life. I give my appreciation to You for the gift of this lifetime.

In Jesus' name, I pray.

Amen.

Suggested Oils: Gratitude, Present Time

Awake

Dear God,

Please guide this oil through my physical body and energy field. Awaken me. Clear my mind. Boost my energy and frequency.

In Jesus' name, I pray.

Amen.

Suggested Oils: Awaken, Brain Power, Clarity, Grounding

Blessings

Dear God,

Please guide this oil through my physical body and energy field. Thank You for all of the blessings that surround me. Thank You for blessing me. Let me be a blessing to others.

In Jesus' name, I pray.

Amen.

Suggested Oils: Abundance, Gratitude, Joy, Rose

Cardiovascular System

Dear God,

Please guide this oil through my physical body and energy field, and to each cell of my body. Support my cardiovascular system, and help me to maintain overall wellness.

In Jesus' name, I pray.

Amen.

Suggested Oils: Aroma Life, Frankincense, Golden Rod, Helichrysum, Rosemary

Career

Dear God,

Please guide this oil through my physical body and energy field. Lead me to work that is in alignment with Your Divine Plan. Bless my work, and let my work be a blessing to others.

In Jesus' name, I pray.

Amen.

Suggested Oils: Highest Potential, Joy, Magnify Your Purpose, Oola Field

Clean Eating

Dear God,

Please help the oils to assist me with my commitment to eating clean. Guide me to nourishing foods that replenish my body. Help me to let go of processed foods. Help me to make time to prepare healthy, wholesome foods as You intended us to eat.

In Jesus' name, I pray.

Amen.

Suggested Oils: Awaken, Lavender, Lemon, Lime, Orange, Peppermint, Spearmint

Clarity

Dear God,

Please guide this oil through my physical body and energy field. Clear my mind, my body, and my energy field. Let my thoughts be clear and divinely guided.

In Jesus' name, I pray.

Amen.

Suggested Oils: Brain Power, Clarity, Release, White Angelica

Connection

Dear God,

Please guide this oil through my physical body and energy field.
Help me to stay connected to You, and to hold a high frequency.
Let me walk in Your Love.

In Jesus' name, I pray.

Amen.

Suggested Oils: Frankincense, Grounding, Sacred Frankincense,
Sacred Mountain

Connecting with My Body

Dear God,

Please guide this oil through my body to help me settle into it
and feel the energy flowing through me. Help me to love and
honor my body. Guide me to foods that nourish and renew my
body.

In Jesus' name, I pray.

Amen.

Suggested Oils: Grounding, Harmony, Lavender, Rose

Creativity

Dear God,

Please guide this oil through my body and energy field to enhance my creativity. Infuse me with energy and love. Help me to express Your Love in physical form. Help me bring comfort and healing to others with my work.

In Jesus' name, I pray.

Amen.

Suggested Oils: Hyssop, Transformation, Wintergreen

Daily Guidance

Dear God,

Please guide this oil through my physical body and energy field. Lead me through my day. Let Your Wisdom attend me in all that I do.

In Jesus' name, I pray.

Amen.

Suggested Oils: Clarity, Grounding, Hong Kuai, Sacred Frankincense

Discernment

Dear God,

Please guide this oil through my physical body and energy field. Help me to see clearly. Infuse me with the Holy Spirit that I may easily discern the truth.

In Jesus' name, I pray.

Amen.

Suggested Oils: Brain Power, Clarity, Exodus II

Divine Timing

Dear God,

Please guide this oil through my physical body and energy field. Help me to align my timing with Divine Timing, and trust that what is for my highest good in alignment with Divine Will is on its way to me.

In Jesus' name, I pray.

Amen.

Suggested Oils: Acceptance, Divine Release, Present Time

Dreams

Dear Heavenly Father,

Please guide this oil through my body and energy field. Help me to bring the dreams you've placed in my heart into reality. Guide my thoughts and actions to create and fulfill my dreams.

In Jesus' name,

Amen.

Suggested Oils: Build Your Dream, Dream Catcher, Highest Potential, Light the Fire

Ears to Hear, Eyes to See

Dear God,

Please guide this oil through my physical body and energy field. Infuse me with the Holy Spirit. Purify my mind, that I may clearly hear You, and easily see the truth.

In Jesus' name, I pray.

Amen.

Suggested Oils: Awaken, Brain Power, Clarity, Grounding, Palo Santo, Present Time, Sacred Frankincense, White Angelica

Energy

Dear God,

Please guide this oil through my body to maintain energy and vitality. Please give me an extra boost of energy and inspiration for the day.

In Jesus' name, I pray.

Amen.

Suggested Oils: Aroma Life, Awaken, En-R-Gee, Motivation, Neroli, Peppermint

Family

Dear God,

Please guide this oil through my physical body and energy field. Protect and shield my family. Keep us connected to each other with love. Help us to maintain a high frequency. Bless my family and all of our loved ones.

In Jesus' name, I pray.

Amen.

Suggested Oils: Gathering, Harmony, Oola Family

Focus

Dear God,

Please guide this oil through my physical body and energy field. Help me daily to stay focused on You. Help me to stay centered and on my path.

In Jesus' name, I pray.

Amen.

Suggested Oils: Clarity, Grounding

Forgiveness

Dear God,

Thank You for the gift of this oil. Please guide this oil through my body and energy field to gently release any past emotions that I may have been harboring. Help me to forgive others and to forgive myself. Help me to release the past and move forward in the light of Your Love.

In Jesus' name,

Amen.

Suggested Oils: Divine Release, Feelings Collection, Forgiveness, Release

Frequency

Dear God,

Please guide this oil through my physical body and energy field. Lift my body and energy field to a high frequency. Help me to hold a high frequency throughout my day and night.

In Jesus' name, I pray.

Amen.

Suggested Oils: Abundance, Exodus II, Forgiveness, Idaho Blue Spruce, Joy, Rose

Gratitude

Dear God,

Please guide this oil through my body and energy field to assist me in seeing all of the beauty around me. Help me to open my heart and express gratitude for the gift of this lifetime.

In Jesus' name,

Amen.

Suggested Oils: Gratitude, Humility

Gratitude for My Body

Dear God,

Please guide this oil through my body and energy field to support harmony in my body. Guide me to self-care that nourishes and replenishes my body and energy field. Help me to feel gratitude and love for all parts of my body and being.

In Jesus' name,

Amen.

Suggested Oils: Gratitude, Grounding, Harmony, Rose

Goals

Dear God,

Please guide this oil through my physical body and energy field. Help me to set goals that are in alignment with my purpose. Guide me as I pursue my goals, and help me to take steps towards them each day.

In Jesus' name, I pray.

Amen.

Suggested Oils: Envision, Magnify Your Purpose, Motivation

Grounding

Dear God,

Please guide this oil through my body and energy field to help me anchor my awareness in my body and in this moment. Help me to feel connected to the earth. Help me to be centered and present.

In Jesus' name, I pray.

Amen.

Suggested Oils: Grounding, Lavender, Peace and Calming, Present Time

Guidance

Dear God,

Please guide this oil through my physical body and energy field. Guide me in all aspects of my life. Help me to navigate each day with ease and joy.

In Jesus' name, I pray.

Amen.

Suggested Oils: Believe, Gathering, Highest Potential, Lavender, Present Time

Harmony

Dear God,

Please guide this oil through my physical body and energy field. Bring me into harmony with my purpose. Infuse my life with harmony.

In Jesus' name, I pray.

Amen.

Suggested Oils: Harmony, Highest Potential, Rose

Heart Centered Business

Dear God,

Please guide this oil through my physical body and energy field. Help me to stay connected with my heart and guide me through business transactions.

In Jesus' name, I pray.

Amen.

Suggested Oils: Harmony, Highest Potential, Rose

Highest Potential

Dear God,

Please guide this oil through my body and energy field. Strengthen and invigorate me. Guide me to my highest path and purpose. Illuminate my next steps to achieve my highest potential.

In Jesus' name, I pray.

Amen.

Suggested Oils: Highest Potential, Sacred Frankincense

Hope

Dear God,

Please guide this oil through my body and energy field. Please help me to connect to You and feel Your Love surrounding me. Restore hope in my heart and illuminate my soul.

In Jesus' name, I pray.

Amen.

Suggested Oils: Hope, Joy, Rose, Valor

Immune System

Dear God,

Please guide this oil through my physical body and energy field. Support my immune system. Protect and shield me. Keep me at a high frequency.

In Jesus' name, I pray.

Amen.

Suggested Oils: Cinnamon Bark, Clove, Orange, Oregano, Thieves

Inspiration

Dear God,

Please guide this oil through my physical body and energy field. Fill me with inspiration and purpose. Infuse me with wellness and abundance. Help me to inspire others to live lives of wellness, purpose, and abundance.

In Jesus' name, I pray.

Amen.

Suggested Oils: Envision, Highest Potential, Inspiration, Motivation

Joy

Dear God,

Please uplift my spirit, mind, and body. Guide the oils through all the cells of my body. Lift me to a higher frequency. Help me radiate joy to everyone around me.

In Jesus' name, I pray.

Amen.

Suggested Oils: Joy, Orange, Rose

Life Purpose

Dear God,

Please guide this oil through my body and energy field. Help me to bring purpose to all aspects of my life. Guide me to the reason I incarnated. Help me to align with my soul and higher purpose for this lifetime. Lift me above daily concerns to see the plan for my life. Guide me to take steps each day towards my higher purpose for this lifetime.

In Jesus' name,

Amen.

Suggested Oils: Believe, Build Your Dream, Envision, Hong Kuai, Magnify Your Purpose, Oola Grow

Love

Dear God,

Please guide this oil through my body and energy field to raise my frequency to the frequency of love. Help me to see that love is present in everything you created. May I radiate love to all beings.

In Jesus' name,

Amen.

Suggested Oils: Joy, Rose

Motivation

Dear God,

Please guide this oil through my physical body and energy field. Help me to stay motivated. Boost my daily energy.

In Jesus' name, I pray.

Amen.

Suggested Oils: En-R-Gee, Hong Kuai, Magnify Your Purpose Motivation, Orange, Peppermint

My Gifts

Dear God,

Please guide this oil through my physical body and energy field. Help me to recognize my gifts and talents, and to use them in alignment with Divine Will. May I enhance this world and express Your Love in all that I do.

In Jesus' name, I pray.

Amen.

Suggested Oils: Clarity, Highest Potential, Magnify Your Purpose, Sacred Frankincense

Passion

Dear God,

Please guide this oil through my physical body and energy field. Please reignite my passion and purpose here on Earth. Help me to infuse all aspects of my life with passion.

In Jesus' name, I pray.

Amen.

Suggested Oils: Aroma Life, Inspiration, Jasmine, Joy, Ylang Ylang

On My Father's Planet

Dear Heavenly Father,

Please guide this oil through my physical body and energy field. Help me to see Your Presence in all of creation. Help me to feel Your Love surrounding me and flowing through me. May I reflect Your Love in all that I do.

In Jesus' name, I pray.

Amen.

Suggested Oils: Clarity, Grounding, Frankincense, Northern Lights Black Spruce, Rose, Sacred Frankincense

Open Heart

Dear God,

Please guide this oil through my physical body and energy field. Open my heart to the love and beauty that surrounds me. Help me to be in each moment and experience the love that flows through and around me.

In Jesus' name, I pray.

Amen.

Suggested Oils: Grounding, Harmony, Joy, Present Time, Rose

Peace

Dear God,

Please guide this oil through my body and energy field. Bring peace to my mind, body, and spirit. Help me to remain centered in love. Help me radiate peace to everyone around me.

In Jesus' name, I pray.

Amen.

Suggested Oils: Lavender, Peace and Calming, Peace and Calming II, Tranquil

Positive Life Changes

Dear God,

Please help me to upgrade my habits and thoughts. Assist me in raising my frequency and taking consistent steps to uplift my life. Illuminate my path and guide me to become the highest version of myself.

In Jesus' name, I pray.

Amen.

Suggested Oils: Aroma Life, Awaken, Divine Release, Motivation, Release, Transformation

Positive Thought

Dear God,

Please guide this oil through my body and energy field. Raise my frequency. Help me to think positive thoughts and speak positive words. Let my thoughts and words be a blessing.

In Jesus' name, I pray.

Amen.

Suggested Oils: Lavender, Orange, Peppermint, Transformation

Present Moment Awareness

Dear God,

Please guide this oil through my body and energy field to help me focus on this moment. Assist me in occupying my body and being centered in the now. Help me to calm my mind and body. Help me resonate with the peace and aliveness of this moment.

In Jesus' name, I pray.

Amen.

Suggested Oils: Grounding, Peace and Calming, Present Time, Stress Away

Prosperity

Dear God,

Please guide this oil through my body and energy field to raise my frequency and increase my prosperity. Thank You for the abundance you have given me. Help me to embrace the unlimited potential that is within me.

In Jesus' name, I pray.

Amen.

Suggested Oils: Abundance, Ginger, Orange

Protection

Dear God,

Please guide this oil through my physical body and energy field. Adorn me with Your Armor. Place a protective energy field around me. Protect and shield me throughout my day and night.

In Jesus' name, I pray.

Amen.

Suggested Oils: Frankincense, Palo Santo, Sacred Frankincense, Valor, Valor II, White Angelica

Protection

Dear God,

Please guide this oil through my physical body and energy field. Fill my living space with the golden light of the Holy Spirit. Protect and shield my living space throughout the day and night.

In Jesus' name, I pray.

Amen.

Suggested Oils: Frankincense, Palo Santo, Sacred Frankincense, White Angelica

Dear God,

Please guide this oil through my physical body and energy field. Help me to maintain a high frequency. Shield and protect me. Shield and protect my family and friends. Surround us with the golden light of the Holy Spirit.

In Jesus' name, I pray.

Amen.

Suggested Oils: Frankincense, Palo Santo, Sacred Frankincense, Valor, Valor II, White Angelica

Purpose

Dear God,

Please guide this oil through my physical body and energy field. Help me to stay focused on my purpose, and spend time each day on my purpose.

In Jesus' name, I pray.

Amen.

Suggested Oils: Envision, Grounding, Magnify Your Purpose

Release

Dear God,

Please guide this oil through my physical body and energy field. Help me to release the past. Please help my cells and cellular memory to release that which no longer serves me. Help me return to peace and harmony.

In Jesus' name, I pray.

Amen.

Suggested Oils: Divine Release, Forgiveness, Present Time, Release, The Feelings Collection, The Freedom Collection

Releasing Trauma

Dear God,

Please guide this oil through my body to help me release the past. Please help my cells and cellular memory to release anything that no longer serves me. Restore my body and energy field to its original blueprint. Help me return to peace and harmony.

In Jesus' name, I pray.

Amen.

Suggested Oils: Divine Release, Forgiveness, Present Time, Release, The Feelings Collection, The Freedom Collection, Valor, Valor II

Rejuvenation

Dear God,

Please guide this oil through my physical body and energy field, and into each cell of my body. Rejuvenate my mind, my body, and soul.

In Jesus' name, I pray.

Amen.

Suggested Oils: Aroma Life, GLF, Helichrysum, Hinoki, ImmuPower, Lavender

Respiratory System

Dear God,

Please guide this oil through my physical body and energy field. Support my respiratory system. Help me to breathe clearly and easily.

In Jesus' name, I pray.

Amen.

Suggested Oils: Eucalyptus (Globulus or Radiata), Frankincense, Helichrysum, Peppermint, Raven, Ravintsara, R.C., Thieves

Sleep

Dear God,

Please help me to gently relax. Guide the oils into the cells of my body. Help me to release the day, and settle into a deep, rejuvenating sleep. Help me to awaken refreshed and revitalized.

In Jesus' name,

Amen.

Suggested Oils: Lavender, Peace and Calming, Peace and Calming II, RutaVaLa, Valerian

Sleep

Dear God,

Please help these oils to gently relax me. Guide them into the cells of my body. Help me to release the day and settle into a deep, rejuvenating sleep, where my body can heal and restore itself.

In Jesus' name, I pray.

Amen.

Suggested Oils: Lavender, Peace and Calming, Peace and Calming II, RutaVaLa, Valerian

Spiritual Connection

Dear God,

Thank You for guiding this oil through me. Raise my frequency to easily connect with You. Let my daily cares fall away, that I may spend this moment fully present and listening to You.

In Jesus' name, I pray.

Amen.

Suggested Oils: Frankincense, Gratitude, Grounding, Inspiration, Oola Faith, Sacred Frankincense, Sacred Mountain

Surrender

Dear God,

Please guide this oil through my physical body and energy field. Help me to surrender that which no longer serves me and step into my full potential.

In Jesus' name, I pray.

Amen.

Suggested Oils: Divine Release, Release, Surrender

Stress

Dear God,

Please guide this oil through my body and energy field. Calm and soothe me. Help me to be grounded and centered in this moment. Help me to know that all is well. Surround me with Your Love and Protection.

In Jesus' name,

Amen.

Suggested Oils: AromaEase, Lavender, Peace and Calming, Peace and Calming II, Stress Away, Tranquil

Synchronicity

Dear God,

Please guide this oil through my physical body and energy field. Help me to recognize synchronicity in my life. Align me with Divine Timing.

In Jesus' name, I pray.

Amen.

Suggested Oils: Grounding, Harmony, Present Time

Synergy

Dear God,

Please guide this oil through my physical body and energy field. Help me to synergize the power of prayer, essential oils, and positivity to maintain a high frequency and enhance my life. Synergize my life with my life's purpose, in alignment with Divine Will.

In Jesus' name, I pray.

Amen.

Suggested Oils: Gathering, Grounding, Harmony, Highest Potential, Sacred Frankincense, Transformation

Thank You

Dear God,

Please guide this oil through my physical body and energy field. Thank You for the blessings You have given me. Thank You for the gift of this lifetime. Thank You for the love that surrounds me.

In Jesus' name, I pray.

Amen.

Suggested Oils: Abundance, Gratitude, Grounding, Present Time

The Gift

Dear God,

Please guide this oil through my physical body and energy field. Thank You for this lifetime. Thank You for Your Love, and Blessings. Thank You for Your Presence and Guidance. Thank You for walking with me in each moment.

I Love You.

In Jesus' name, I pray.

Amen.

Suggested Oils: Gratitude, Joy, Present Time, Rose, Sacred Frankincense, The Gift

Time

Dear God,

Please guide this oil through my physical body and energy field. Assist me with budgeting my time wisely. Align my priorities with my purpose and help me make the best use of my time.

In Jesus' name, I pray.

Amen.

Suggested Oils: Brain Power, Clarity, Grounding, Present Time

Trust

Dear God,

Please guide this oil through my physical body and energy field. Help me to trust that everything is in alignment with Divine Will. Raise my frequency and help me to walk in love.

In Jesus' name,

Amen.

Suggested Oils: Believe, Idaho Blue Spruce, Rose, Transformation

Truth

Dear God,

Please guide this oil through my physical body and energy field. Clear my mind. Infuse me with the Holy Spirit. Lead me to see the truth in all matters.

In Jesus' name, I pray.

Amen.

Suggested Oils: Brain Power, Clarity, Grounding, Sacred Frankincense, White Angelica

Transformation

Dear God,

Please help this oil to release anything that no longer serves me. Help me transform into the highest version of myself. Please protect and guide me through this transformation.

In Jesus' name,

Amen.

Suggested Oils: Divine Release, Release, Transformation

Unconditional Love

Dear God,

Please guide this oil through my physical body and energy field.
Raise my frequency and help me to feel Your Love for me.
Guide me in loving others unconditionally.

In Jesus' name, I pray.

Amen.

Suggested Oils: Divine Release, Joy, Rose

Walking My Path

Dear God,

Please guide this oil through my physical body and energy field.
Light my path and guide me daily. Help me to walk my path,
and be a shining example of Your Love.

In Jesus' name, I pray.

Amen.

Suggested Oils: Awaken, Build Your Dream, Clarity, Valor

Walking with Our Savior

Dear God,

Please guide this oil through my physical body and energy field. Connect me with my Savior, Jesus Christ, and lead me to walk daily with Him.

In Jesus' name, I pray.

Amen.

Suggested Oils: Frankincense, Sacred Frankincense

Wellness

Dear God,

Please guide these oils through my body and energy field. Balance my body and support vibrant wellness.

In Jesus' name,

Amen.

Suggested Oils: Copaiba, Lemon, Lemon Myrtle, Lime, Orange, Neroli

Wellness

Dear God,

Please guide these oils through my body and energy field. Raise my frequency and support my digestive system and my immune system. Please rejuvenate and refresh me.

In Jesus' name,

Amen.

Suggested Oils: Copaiba, Digize, Rose, Thieves

Dear God,

Please guide these oils through my body and energy field. Thank You that all is well with me.

In Jesus' name,

Amen.

Suggested Oils: Abundance, Gratitude, Joy, Northern Lights Black Spruce, Rose

Single Oils

Cypress

Dear God,

Please guide this oil - Cypress - through my body and energy field. Support my circulatory system. Please help me to be grounded and heal my emotions.

In Jesus' name, I pray.

Amen.

Frankincense

Dear God,

Please guide this blessed oil - Frankincense - through my body and energy field. Support vibrant wellness throughout my mind, body, and soul.

In Jesus' name, I pray.

Amen.

Helichrysum

Dear God,

Please guide this oil - Helichrysum - through my body and
energy field. Regenerate my body and aura. Uplift me.

In Jesus' name, I pray.

Amen.

Idaho Balsam Fir

Dear God,

Please guide this oil – Idaho Balsam Fir - through my body and
energy field. Balance my body and calm my emotions.

In Jesus' name, I pray.

Amen.

Lavender

Dear God,

Please guide this oil - Lavender - through my body and energy
field. Guide the oil to where it is most needed. Bless me, and let
me be a blessing to others.

In Jesus' name, I pray.

Amen.

Lavender

Dear God,

Please guide this gentle oil of Lavender through my body. Help me relax and let go of stress.

In Jesus' name,

Amen.

Lavender

Dear God,

Please guide this Lavender oil through all aspects of me. Restore and rejuvenate me, and prepare me for a deep, restful night of sleep.

In Jesus' name,

Amen.

Lemon

Dear God,

Please guide Lemon essential oil through my body and energy field. Help me to gently cleanse and detox my body. Please assist me with shifting to healthy choices.

In Jesus' name,

Amen.

Neroli

Dear God,

Please guide this oil – Neroli – through my body and energy field. Surround me with its fragrance. Calm my emotions. Help me to focus and be energized.

In Jesus' name,

Amen.

Northern Lights Black Spruce

Dear God,

Please guide this oil – Northern Lights Black Spruce- through my body and energy field. Infuse me with the electrical charge of the Northern Lights. Surround me with the fragrance of the woods.

In Jesus' name, I pray.

Amen.

Ocotea

Dear God,

Please guide this oil – Ocotea – through my body and energy field. Cleanse and restore all of my cells to vibrant wellness.

In Jesus' Name,

Amen.

Orange

Dear God,

Please guide Orange oil through my body and energy field. Support my immune system and uplift me.

In Jesus' Name,

Amen.

Peppermint

Dear God,

Please guide this oil - Peppermint – through my body and energy field. Energize and uplift me. Please help the oil to clear my mind and refresh me.

In Jesus' Name,

Amen.

Peppermint

Dear God,

Please guide this oil - Peppermint - through my body and energy field. Please calm and soothe my digestive system.

In Jesus' name, I pray.

Amen.

Rose

Dear God,

Please guide Rose oil through my body to bathe each of my cells in love. Help me to raise my frequency to the frequency of love. Help me to radiate love to others.

In Jesus' Name, I pray.

Amen.

Sacred Frankincense

Dear God,

Please guide this blessed oil – Sacred Frankincense - through my body and energy field. Deepen my connection with You. May I walk each day with You.

In Jesus' name, I pray.

Amen.

Ylang Ylang

Dear God,

Please guide this oil – Ylang Ylang – through my body and energy field to soothe and uplift me. Shield me and surround me with positive frequencies. Bring balance to my body and emotions.

In Jesus' Name, I pray.

Amen.

Affirmations

Abundance

I am open to receiving Abundance.

I accept Abundance.

I deserve Abundance.

I choose to have Abundance.

I create Abundance!

I create Financial Abundance!

I receive and accept Abundance.

I have Abundance.

I vibrate at the frequency of Abundance!

Suggested Oils: Abundance, Ginger, Gratitude, Orange

Acceptance

I accept the present moment.

I choose to accept the present moment

I accept myself.

I choose to accept myself.

I accept my life.

I accept love.

I accept Divine Love.

Suggested Oils: Acceptance, Harmony, Rose

Affirmation

I affirm the blessings in my life.

I affirm my life.

I affirm a high frequency!

I affirm that I am blessed.

I affirm my prosperity.

I affirm the good in my life.

Suggested Oils: Aroma Life, Awaken, Grounding

Ageless

I choose to be ageless.

I am ageless.

I am radiant.

I hold positive energy!

I choose to hold positive energy!

I hold positive thoughts.

I choose to hold positive thoughts.

Suggested Oils: Cedarwood, Frankincense, Helichrysum, Myrrh, Sacred Frankincense

Alignment

I am in alignment.

I am in alignment with Divine Will.

I choose to be in alignment.

I choose to be in alignment with Divine Will.

My life is in alignment with Divine Will.

My life is in alignment with my life purpose.

My body is in alignment.

I am aligned with my purpose.

I am aligned with wellness.

I am aligned with prosperity.

Suggested Oils: Grounding, Highest Potential, Magnify Your Purpose, Raindrop Collection, Valor, Valor II

Angels

Angels surround me.

Angels surround my house.

Angels walk with me.

Suggested Oils: Angelica, Sacred Frankincense, White Angelica

Appreciation

I appreciate myself.

I appreciate my partner.

I appreciate my life.

I appreciate my income.

I appreciate my time.

I appreciate my talents.

I appreciate my family.

I appreciate my friends.

I appreciate having multiple incomes.

Suggested Oils: Gratitude, Present Time

Attention

I place my attention on what I want.

I focus my attention on what I want more of.

Suggested Oils: Brain Power, Clarity, Grounding, Joy

Awake

I choose to be awake.

I am awake.

I am present and awake.

I choose to be present and awake.

Awaken me.

Suggested Oils: Awaken, Present Time

Balance

My body is balanced.

The systems of my body are balanced.

All areas of my life are balanced.

My hormones are balanced.

I am balanced.

Suggested Oils: Oola Balance, Peace and Calming, Peace and Calming II, Valor, Valor II

Being

I allow others to be themselves.

I allow myself to be.

Suggested Oils: Forgiveness, Grounding, Rose

Belief

I believe.

I believe I can.

I believe in myself.

I believe in my dreams.

I believe I can create my dreams.

I believe I can achieve my dreams.

I believe I am Divinely guided.

I believe I can change my thoughts.

I believe I can change my life.

Suggested Oils: Believe, Build Your Dream, Envision

Boundaries

I know when to create boundaries.

I create healthy boundaries.

Suggested Oils: Palo Santo, Valor, Valor II, White Angelica

Business

My business is blessed.

My business is a blessing to me.

I bless others through my business.

My business transactions are Divinely guided.

Suggested Oils: Highest Potential, Joy, Magnify Your Purpose, Oola Field

Calm

I am calm.

I am connected to the earth.

I am connected to my center.

I hold a calming energy.

Suggested Oils: Idaho Balsam Fir, Grounding, Lavender, Peace and Calming, Peace and Calming II, Spearmint

Career

I choose to love my current job.

My career is Divinely guided.

My work is a blessing.

May my coworkers be blessed.

I choose to do my job with excellence.

Suggested Oils: Highest Potential, Joy, Magnify Your Purpose, Oola Field

Celebration

I celebrate this moment.

I choose to celebrate this moment.

Suggested Oils: Christmas Spirit, Joy

Centered

I am centered.

I am centered and balanced.

I am connected with my center.

Suggested Oils: Grounding, Peace and Calming, Peace and Calming II, Present Time

Change

Change is easy.

I choose to make change easy.

I choose to make change fun.

I embrace new possibilities.

Suggested Oils: Awaken, Into the Future, Oola Grow, Transformation

Cherish

I cherish myself.

I cherish my loved ones.

I cherish others.

I cherish my work.

I cherish this lifetime.

I cherish each moment.

I cherish time with loved ones.

I cherish each new day.

Suggested Oils: Gratitude, Joy

Christmas Spirit

I am surrounded by joy throughout the year.

I am surrounded by love throughout the year.

The feeling of love is with me each day.

The feeling of Christmas is with me all year.

The feeling of Christmas is with me each day.

Suggested Oils: Christmas Spirit, Joy

Clarity

My mind and energy field are clear.

My energy field is clear.

It is easy for me to think clearly.

My mind is clear and focused.

I am clear.

I choose to be clear.

I am clear on my direction.

My path is clear.

I think clearly.

Suggested Oils: Brain Power, Clarity, Peppermint, Rosemary

Clean Eating

I choose foods that nourish my body.

I choose foods that support my body.

It's easy for me to eat clean.

I am upgrading my food choices.

I eat whole foods that nourish me.

I choose to meal plan.

I choose to buy healthy, nourishing food.

Suggested Oils: Awaken, Lavender, Lemon, Lime, Orange, Peppermint, Spearmint

Compassion

I choose to be compassionate.

I am compassionate.

I look upon others with compassion.

Suggested Oils: Rose

Confidence

I am confident.

I choose to be confident.

I speak with confidence.

I move with confidence.

Suggested Oils: Jasmine, Valor, Valor II

Connection

I am connected with my purpose.

I am connected with my Creator.

I am connected with my partner.

I am connected with my family.

I am connected with my friends.

I am connected with nature.

I am connected with this moment.

Suggested Oils: Aroma Life, Clarity, Grounding, Present Time

Connection with My Body

I listen to my body.

I nurture my body.

I am present in my body.

I nourish my body with healthy, energizing foods.

I love my body.

I appreciate my body.

I honor my body.

I am grateful for my body.

I am connected with my body.

Suggested Oils: Grounding, Harmony, Rose, Stress Away

Consistency

I take consistent action toward my dreams.

I consistently spend time pursuing my dreams.

I take consistent action towards my goals.

I consistently spend time on my goals.

Suggested Oils: Build Your Dream, Envision, Motivation

Courage

I have the courage I need.

I choose to be courageous.

I am courageous.

Suggested Oils: Valor, Valor II

Create

I create the life I want.

I choose to create the life I want.

I create healing.

I choose to create healing.

I create abundance.

I choose to create abundance.

I create joy.

I choose to create joy.

I create harmony.

I choose to create harmony.

I create transformation.

I choose to create transformation.

I create a safe space.

I choose to create a safe space.

I create prosperity.

I choose to create prosperity.

I create love.

I choose to create love.

All of my creations are in alignment with Divine Will.

I create _____.

I choose to create _____.

Suggested Oils: Highest Potential, Hyssop, Transformation, Wintergreen

Creativity

Infuse my creations with passion.

Infuse me with energy and love.

Help me to bring healing through my work.

Light my creative fire.

Suggested Oils: Hyssop, Light the Fire, Transformation, Wintergreen

Destiny

I choose to know my destiny.

I know my destiny.

Suggested Oils: Magnify Your Purpose

Digestive System

My digestive system is well.

My digestive system is calm.

My digestive system is strong.

I eat foods that support my digestive system.

I choose to have a strong digestive system.

I eat foods that nourish me.

Suggested Oils: Basil, Digize, Fennel, Ginger, Peppermint

Discernment

I easily discern the truth.

I easily discern the correct choice.

I easily discern the best path.

I easily discern the right action.

I easily discern what is the best for me.

Suggested Oils: Brain Power, Clarity, Exodus II

Divine Guidance

I am Divinely guided.

I am Divinely guided in my choices.

Suggested Oils: Clarity, Grounding, Hong Kuai, Sacred Frankincense

Divine Timing

My timing is in alignment with Divine Timing.

I trust Divine Timing.

I align with Divine Timing.

I am aligned with Divine Timing.

Suggested Oils: Acceptance, Divine Release, Present Time

Dreams

I choose to bring my dreams into reality.

I am pursuing my dreams.

I create my dreams.

I create my life.

I focus my energy on my dreams.

Suggested Oils: Build Your Dream, Dream Catcher

Driving

Path of white light from me to my destination.

My vehicle on that path of light.

Golden Light of the Holy Spirit around my vehicle.

Angels protect me when I'm driving.

Suggested Oils: Frankincense, Palo Santo, Sacred Frankincense, White Angelica

Ears to Hear

Open my mind to hear the truth.

I am Divinely guided to what I need to hear.

I listen with discernment.

I listen with love.

Suggested Oils: Helichrysum, Lavender, Peppermint

Ease

I move with ease.

I create what I want with ease and grace.

It's easy for me to change.

I create what I want with ease.

I learn with ease.

I work with ease and grace.

Suggested Oils: Brain Power, Clarity, Oola Grow, Transformation

Elevate

I elevate my thoughts.

I elevate my focus.

I elevate my frequency!

I elevate my work.

I elevate my life.

Suggested Oils: Abundance, Highest Potential, Joy, Northern Lights Black Spruce, Rose

Energy

I have energy.

I have the energy I need.

I eat foods that support vibrant energy.

My energy is increasing!

Suggested Oils: Aroma Life, Awaken, En-R-Gee, Motivation, Neroli, Peppermint

Energy Field

My energy field is clear.

My energy field vibrates at a high frequency!

My energy field is filled with the golden light of the Holy Spirit.

I create a positive energy field.

Suggested Oils: Abundance, Highest Potential, Joy, Ledum, Northern Lights Black Spruce, Rose, White Angelica

Eyes to See

My eyes are open to see clearly.

My eyes are open to see the truth.

I see with discernment.

I look upon things with love.

I look upon others with love.

I look upon myself with love.

Suggested Oils: Aroma Life, Clarity, 3 Wise Men

Evaluation

I take time to evaluate my life.

I evaluate my goals.

I evaluate what I spend my time on.

I evaluate what I spend my money on.

I evaluate my priorities.

I evaluate my thoughts.

Suggested Oils: Clarity, Envision, Into the Future, Present Time

Excellence

I do everything with excellence.

I choose to do things with excellence.

I choose to be excellent.

I infuse my work with excellence.

Suggested Oils: Brain Power, Clarity, Grounding

Family

My family is blessed.

My family is protected.

My family is a blessing.

Suggested Oils: Abundance, Harmony, Oola Family

Feelings

It is easy for me to let go of past feelings.

It's easy for me to feel my emotions and let them go.

I let go of that which no longer serves me.

I acknowledge my feelings.

Suggested Oils: Divine Release, Feelings Collection, Release

Focus

I am focused.

I choose to be focused.

I focus on the positive.

I choose to focus on the positive.

I focus my thoughts on what I want.

I focus my thoughts on what I want more of.

I focus my energy on what I want.

I focus my energy on what I want more of.

I focus my emotions on what I want.

I focus on love.

I focus on joy.

I focus on abundance.

Suggested Oils: Brain Power, Clarity, Grounding, Peace and Calming, Peace and Calming II, Peppermint

Forgiveness

I forgive myself.

I forgive others.

I forgive and release that which no longer serves me.

Suggested Oils: Feelings Collection, Forgiveness, Release

Freedom

I choose to be free.

I am free.

I am free from the past.

I am free to be happy.

I am free to have vibrant wellness.

I choose to have time freedom.

I choose to have financial freedom.

Suggested Oils: Awaken, Freedom Collection Bundle, Release

Frequency

I choose to hold a high frequency!

My body holds a high frequency!

My energy field holds a high frequency!

My thoughts are a high frequency!

I maintain a high frequency throughout my day!

I maintain a high frequency throughout my night!

My living space is at a high frequency!

Suggested Oils: Abundance, Idaho Blue Spruce, Joy, Northern Lights Black Spruce, Rose

Friends

I am grateful for my friends.

Bless and protect my friends.

Surround my friends with love.

Surround my friends with Divine Love.

Suggested Oils: Oola Friends

Gathering

I gather my energy and focus on what I want.

I gather my family's energies to be united and harmonious.

I gather my team's energies to be a united and thriving group.

Suggested Oils: Gathering

Gifts

I recognize my gifts.

I am using my gifts.

I am using my gifts in alignment with my purpose.

I am using my gifts in alignment with Divine Will.

Suggested Oils: Magnify Your Purpose, Oola Field

Goals

I set specific goals for myself.

I budget time to work on my goals.

My goals are Divinely guided.

My goals are in alignment with my life purpose.

Suggested Oils: Envision, Magnify Your Purpose, Motivation

Gratitude

I am grateful.

I am grateful for this lifetime.

I am grateful for _____.

Suggested Oils: Gratitude

Grounding

I am grounded.

I choose to be grounded.

I am grounded and present.

I choose to be grounded and present.

I am connected with the earth.

Suggested Oils: Grounding, Lavender, Peace and Calming, Peace and Calming II, Present Time

Growth

Personal growth is easy.

Personal growth is exciting.

I take responsibility for myself.

I take responsibility for my growth.

Suggested Oils: Oola Grow, Transformation

Happiness

I choose to be happy.

I create happiness.

I am happy.

I resonate with happiness.

I radiate happiness.

Suggested Oils: Christmas Spirit, Joy, Orange

Harmony

I am in harmony with life.

I am in harmony with my purpose.

I am in harmony with Divine Guidance.

I create harmony.

My relationships are harmonious.

I resonate with harmony.

Suggested Oils: Harmony

Heart Centered Business

I am connected with my heart.

My business is Divinely guided.

I am connected with my heart while doing business.

I am Divinely inspired in my business.

My business is infused with love.

I speak from my heart.

I listen with my heart.

Suggested Oils: Harmony, Highest Potential, Rose

Highest Potential

I know my highest potential.

I operate from my highest potential.

I commit to living my highest potential.

I take consistent action to reach my highest potential.

Suggested Oils: Highest Potential, Sacred Frankincense

Holding Space

I hold space for healing.

I hold space for my healing.

I hold space for others to heal.

I create a healing environment.

Suggested Oils: Angelica, Believe, Forgiveness, Frankincense, Joy, Sacred Frankincense, Rose

Honor

I honor God.

I honor myself.

I honor my time.

Suggested Oils: Present Time

Hope

Restore hope in my heart.

Let me feel God's Love surrounding me.

Suggested Oils: Hope, Joy, Rose, Valor, Valor II

I Am

I am well.

I am loved.

I am prosperous.

I am that I am.

I am inspired.

I am _____.

Suggested Oils: Joy, Northern Lights Black Spruce, Sacred Frankincense, Rose

I Can

I can.

I can have _____.

I can create this.

I can do this.

I can finish this.

I can do anything I choose to do.

Suggested Oils: Envision, Motivation, Oola Balance, Valor, Valor II

Immune System

My immune system is strong.

I eat foods that support my immune system.

I am in a state of continual wellness.

I vibrate at the frequency of wellness!

Suggested Oils: Cinnamon Bark, Clove, Orange, Oregano, Thieves

Infused

I am infused with grace.

I am infused with love.

I am infused with joy.

I am infused with energy!

I am infused with inspiration.

I am infused with the Holy Spirit.

Suggested Oils: Infused 7 kit, Joy, Rose, Sacred Frankincense

Inner Guidance

I hear my inner guidance.

I easily hear my inner guidance.

I listen to my inner guidance.

I choose to listen to my inner guidance.

Suggested Oils: Gathering, Grounding, Sacred Frankincense

Inspiration

I am inspired.

I choose to be inspired.

My work is inspired.

Suggested Oils: Inspiration

Intention

I intend to walk in love.

I intend to be successful.

I intend to be happy.

I intend to have prosperity.

I intend to be loved.

Suggested Oils: Envision, Magnify Your Purpose

Intuition

I listen to my intuition.

I choose to listen to my intuition.

I trust my intuition.

I choose to trust my intuition.

I follow my intuition.

I choose to follow my intuition.

Suggested Oils: Gathering, Grounding, Sacred Frankincense

Joy

I hold the energy of joy.

I hold the frequency of joy!

I am joyful.

I radiate joy.

I experience joy.

I resonate with joy.

Suggested Oils: Joy, Orange, Rose

Knowing

I know my path.

I know.

I choose to know.

I trust my knowing.

Suggested Oils: Clarity, Magnify Your Purpose, Peppermint

Life Purpose

I am aligned with my life purpose.

I align my thoughts with my purpose.

My purpose is clear.

I recognize my purpose.

Suggested Oils: Believe, Build Your Dream, Clarity, Envision, Grounding, Hong Kuai, Magnify Your Purpose, Oola Grow

Love

I am love.

I am loved.

Love flows through me.

I radiate love.

I create love!

I vibrate at the frequency of love!

Suggested Oils: Joy, Rose

Money

I have extra money.

I deserve to have extra money.

I choose to have extra money.

I am increasing my income.

I am increasing my income each month.

I am increasing my income each week.

I am increasing my income by _____* each week.

I have extra money each week.

I have enough money.

I have more than enough money.

I have an abundance of money.

*Be specific. By $10, $50, $100, $500 or a percent 1%, 5%, 10%, 25% etc. Start with an amount your subconscious mind will believe, and then increase it as you increase your belief.

Suggested Oils: Abundance, Ginger, Orange

Movement

I incorporate movement into each day.

I know what movement supports my body.

I listen to my body.

I know what movement supports wellness.

I choose to make time for movement.

Suggested Oils: Oola Fitness

Moving Forward

It is easy for me to move forward.

It's easy for me to let go of the past.

I have the courage to move forward.

I have energy to move forward.

Suggested Oils: Into the Future, Release

Motivation

I am motivated.

I choose to be motivated.

I choose to be self-motivated.

I keep my commitments to myself.

I renegotiate my commitments to myself when necessary.

Suggested Oils: En-R-Gee, Hong Kuai, Magnify Your Purpose, Motivation, Orange, Peppermint

My Body

I nurture my body.

I appreciate my body.

I am kind to my body.

I love my body.

I accept my body.

Suggested Oils: Grounding, Harmony, Present Time, Rose

My Cells

My cells are programmed for wellness.

My cells are programmed for financial abundance.

My cells are programmed to hold a high frequency!

My cells hold a high frequency!

My cells are bathed in love.

My cells are programmed for success.

My cells are programmed for life!

Suggested Oils: Abundance, Aroma Life, Idaho Blue Spruce, Joy, Northern Lights Black Spruce, Rose

Nature

I spend time in nature.

I spend time outdoors.

Suggested Oils: Northern Lights Black Spruce

Nurturing

I take time to nurture myself.

I create a nurturing environment.

I know what nurtures me.

I nourish my mind.

I nourish my body.

I nourish my soul.

I deserve to be nurtured.

Suggested Oils: Grounding, Lavender, Peace and Calming, Peace and Calming II, Present Time, Stress Away

Organization

I choose to be organized.

It's easy for me to be organized.

I am organized.

Suggested Oils: Clarity, Motivation

Passion

My life is infused with passion.

My work is infused with passion.

Suggested Oils: Aroma Life, Inspiration, Jasmine, Joy, Live with Passion, Ylang, Ylang

Patience

I have patience.

I choose to have patience.

I am patient.

I choose to be patient.

Suggested Oils: Lavender, Peace and Calming, Peace and Calming II

Peace

I resonate with peace.

I create a peaceful environment.

I hold the frequency of peace.

Suggested Oils: Lavender, Peace and Calming, Peace and Calming II, Stress Away, Tranquil

Positive Emotions

I focus on my positive emotions.

I choose to have positive emotions.

I guide my emotions to the positive.

Suggested Oils: Awaken, Christmas Spirit, Joy, Orange, Release

Positive Life Changes

I choose to make positive life changes.

I embrace positive life changes.

I vibrate at a positive frequency!

I create a positive environment.

Suggested Oils: Aroma Life, Awaken, Divine Release, Motivation, Oola Grow, Release, Transformation

Positive Thoughts

I focus on the positive.

I choose to think positive thoughts.

I choose my thoughts wisely.

My thoughts are a blessing.

I redirect my thoughts to the positive. (as many times as needed)

I think positive thoughts.

I think positive thoughts throughout my day.

Suggested Oils: Lavender, Orange, Peppermint, Transformation

Positive Words

I speak positive words.

My words are a blessing.

My words bless me.

My words bless others.

Suggested Oils: Awaken, Envision, Joy

Power

I take my power back.

I choose to take my power back.

Suggested Oils: Valor, Valor II

Present Moment

I am present.

I am present in this moment.

I choose to be present.

I choose to be present in this moment.

Suggested Oils: Grounding, Peace and Calming, Peace and
Calming II, Present Time, Stress Away

Prosperity

I have multiple streams of income.

I am creating prosperity in my life.

I am creating prosperity.

I am prosperous.

I am open and receptive of prosperity.

I vibrate at the frequency of prosperity!

I attract prosperity.

I choose to be prosperous.

Suggested Oils: Abundance, Ginger, Orange

Protection

I am shielded and protected.

I am surrounded by the golden light of the Holy Spirit.

My living space is shielded and protected.

My living space is filled with the golden light of the Holy Spirit.

Angels surround and protect my living space.

Suggested Oils: Frankincense, Palo Santo, Sacred Frankincense, White Angelica, Valor, Valor II

Purification

I choose to have pure thoughts.

My mind is purified.

My body is purified.

My environment is purified.

Suggested Oils: Purification, White Angelica

Radiance

I am radiant.

I choose to be radiant.

I radiate Divine Love.

Suggested Oils: Joy, Rose

Reflection

I take time to reflect on my purpose.

I take time to reflect on my life.

I take time to reflect on my priorities.

I spend time in reflection.

Suggested Oils: Grounding, Peace and Calming, Peace and Calming II, Present Time, Stress Away

Rejuvenation

I choose to be rejuvenated.

It's easy for me to rejuvenate.

My cells are being rejuvenated.

My body is continually rejuvenated.

Suggested Oils: Aroma Life, GLF, Helichrysum, Hinoki, ImmuPower, Lavender

Relationships

My relationships are harmonious.

My relationships are positive.

My relationships are supportive.

I treasure my relationships.

Suggested Oils: Harmony, Joy, Oola Family, Oola Friends

Relaxation

I breathe in peace.

I breathe deeply and center myself.

I am relaxed.

I choose to be relaxed.

Suggested Oils: Lavender, Peace and Calming, Peace and
Calming II, Stress Away

Resonance

I resonate with my purpose.

I resonate with love.

I resonate.

I resonate with life.

I resonate with Divine Wisdom.

I resonate with Divine Love.

I resonate with Divine Order.

I resonate with Divine Timing.

I resonate with Divine Truth.

Suggested Oils: Harmony, Joy, Northern Lights Black Spruce, Rose

Respiratory System

I breathe with ease.

Suggested Oils: Eucalyptus (Globulus or Radiata), Frankincense, Helichrysum, Peppermint, Raven, Ravinstara, R.C., Thieves

Responsibility

I choose to be responsible.

I am responsible.

I choose to be responsible for my life.

I am responsible for my life.

I choose to be responsible for my wellness.

I am responsible for my wellness.

I choose to be responsible for my finances.

I am responsible for my finances.

Suggested Oils: Clarity, Grounding, Present Time

Restful Sleep

I release the day.

I awaken refreshed from sleeping.

It's easy for me to fall asleep.

I relax into restful sleep.

Suggested Oils: Lavender, Peace and Calming, Peace and Calming II, RutaVaLa, Valerian

Secure

I am safe.

I am secure.

Suggested Oils: Valor, Valor II

Self-Awareness

I choose to be self-aware.

I am self-aware.

Suggested Oils: Grounding, Oola Grow, Present Time

Self-Love

I choose to love myself.

I love myself.

I treat myself with love.

I allow love to flow through me.

I accept God's Love for me.

Suggested Oils: Believe, Grounding, Joy, Rose

Self-Worth

I am worthy.

I know that I am worthy.

I feel that I am worthy.

I deserve to exist.

I deserve love.

I am falling in love with myself.

Suggested Oils: Rose, Valor, Valor II

Serenity

I hold serene energy.

I create a serene energy field.

I create a serene living space.

I create a serene work space.

Suggested Oils: Lavender, Peace and Calming, Peace and Calming II, Stress Away, Tranquil

Service

I am Divinely guided in my service.

I use my talents as a form of service.

Suggested Oils: Sacred Frankincense, Surrender

Spiritual Connection

Help me to easily connect with You.

It's easy for me to stay connected.

I spend time listening for guidance.

Suggested Oils: Frankincense, Gratitude, Grounding, Inspiration, Oola Faith, Sacred Frankincense, Sacred Mountain

Spontaneity

I embrace spontaneity.

It's easy for me to be flexible.

It's easy for me to be in the moment.

I leave space for the Divine.

Suggested Oils: Aroma Life, Live with Passion, Surrender

Strength

I am strong.

I choose to be strong.

I walk away from that which no longer serves me.

I am infused with strength.

Suggested Oils: Valor, Valor II

Success

I choose to be successful.

I am successful.

I create success!

I vibrate at the frequency of success!

Suggested Oils: Abundance, Oola Field, Oola Finance

Support

I am supported.

I am supported in all aspects of my life.

Suggested Oils: Aroma Life, Envision

Surrender

I surrender.

I choose to surrender.

I surrender _____.

Suggested Oils: Surrender

Synchronicity

I vibrate at the frequency of synchronicity!

I recognize synchronicity.

Suggested Oils: Grounding, Harmony, Present Time

Synergy

I am synergized.

I synergize my life.

I synergize my work.

I create with synergy.

Suggested Oils: Gathering, Grounding, Harmony, Highest Potential, Sacred Frankincense, Transformation

The Gift

Thank You for this lifetime.

Suggested Oils: Gratitude, Joy, Present Time, Rose, Sacred Frankincense, The Gift

Time

I budget my time wisely.

I use my time wisely.

I spend time doing what I love.

I invest time in myself.

I budget time for my top priorities.

I spend time with loved ones.

I invest time on my calling.

Suggested Oils: Brain Power, Clarity, Grounding, Present Time

Transformation

I choose to transform.

It's easy for me to transform.

Transformation is exciting!

Suggested Oils: Divine Release, Release, Transformation

Travel

I have extra money to travel.

I am Divinely guided in my travels.

I am inspired by traveling.

My travel plans go smoothly.

Suggested Oils: Abundance, Inspiration, Thieves, Valor, Valor II, White Angelica

Trust

I trust myself.

I trust God.

I trust the Universe.

Suggested Oils: Believe

Truth

I easily know the truth.

I recognize the truth.

Suggested Oils: Brain Power, Clarity, Grounding, Sacred Frankincense, White Angelica

Unconditional Love

I vibrate at the frequency of unconditional love!

I love unconditionally.

I resonate with unconditional love.

Suggested Oils: Divine Release, Release, Joy, Rose

Upgrading

I choose to upgrade how I spend my time.

I am upgrading how I spend my time.

I choose to upgrade my thoughts.

I am upgrading my thoughts.

I choose to upgrade my life.

I am upgrading my life.

I am upgrading my habits.

Suggested Oils: Awaken, Grounding, Present Time

Value

I bring value to everything I do.

I value myself.

I value my time.

I value other's time.

Suggested Oils: Grounding, Harmony, Present Time

Vibration

I hold a high vibration!

My living space is at a high vibration!

I have a positive vibration!

Suggested Oils: Abundance, Joy, Northern Lights Black Spruce, Rose

Walking in Light

I walk in Divine Light.

I choose to walk in the light.

My life is infused with light.

Suggested Oils: Northern Lights Black Spruce, Rose, Sacred Frankincense

Walking in Love

I walk in love.

Divine Love flows through me.

Suggested Oils: Joy, Rose

Walking My Path

I know my path.

I am focused on my path.

I am walking my path.

Suggested Oils: Build Your Dream, Magnify Your Purpose, Oola Field

Wellness

I am well.

I choose wellness.

I choose to be well.

My cells are programmed for wellness.

All is well.

Suggested Oils: Copaiba, Digize, ImmuPower, Lemon, Lemon Myrtle, Lime, Orange, Neroli, Rose, Thieves

Wholeness

I am whole.

I use a whole brain approach.

Suggested Oils: Brain Power, Clarity, Gathering, Harmony

Wisdom

I am infused with wisdom.

Wisdom attends me.

I am infused with Divine Wisdom.

Suggested Oils: Grounding, Present Time, Sacred Frankincense

Conclusion

Remember to be gentle with yourself, but also intentional with where you place your thoughts and focus. Keep your thoughts and energy positive. Infuse what you want with positive emotion. Keep single pointed focus on what you want to bring into your life.

Allow the oils, prayers, and affirmations to help you shift your consciousness and upgrade your life. Keep guiding your thoughts and emotions to the positive, until positivity becomes your natural state of being. Embrace the blessings that will enter into your life, and enjoy the ability to be a blessing to others.

I hope that the time spent in prayer and reflection while applying the oils has brought you to a deeper connection with yourself and with God. Life is a gift and is meant to be enjoyed. Being present and aware of this moment helps you to experience the fullness of the moment and of life. Being present in your body makes it easier to be in the present moment versus thinking about the past or always focusing on the future. The best way to create the future you want is to be fully present now.

Connecting with God daily also helps you to be in the present moment and fully appreciate your time here on Earth. Staying connected to God also helps to maintain a high frequency and a clear energy field. A clear mind, body, and energy field helps create wellness, purpose, and abundance. Living a lifestyle that supports wellness, purpose, and abundance will help you to fulfill your purpose here. A life in alignment with your soul brings true fulfillment and success.

May you walk in love, peace and joy.

Love and Blessings,

Jennie M. Fuller

YL Member #1757073

Website: www.ylbewell.com

Email: jenniefuller1@gmail.com

Suggested Reading

Essential Oils Desk Reference

 or Pocket Reference book by Life Science Publishing

Healing Oils of the Bible by David Stewart, Ph.D.

The Chemistry of Essential Oils Made Simple: God's Love Manifest in Molecules by David Steward, Ph.D.

The One Gift by D. Gary Young

Additional copies of this book are available on Amazon or Createspace at: https://www.createspace.com/6558691

Please note that this book – Moments of Reflection – contains all of the prayers from Moments of Connection and all of the affirmations from Moments of Affirmation.

Moments of Connection – Prayers to accompany essential oils is available on Amazon or Createspace at: https://www.createspace.com/5966682

Moments of Affirmation to Accompany Essential Oils is available on Amazon or Createspace at: https://www.createspace.com/6089062

Connect with me on Facebook at Moments of Connection page:

https://www.facebook.com/momentsofconnection/